Red R
Hoc

A ZEBRA BOOK

Retold by Wendy Boase
Illustrated by Heather Philpott

PUBLISHED BY
WALKER BOOKS
LONDON

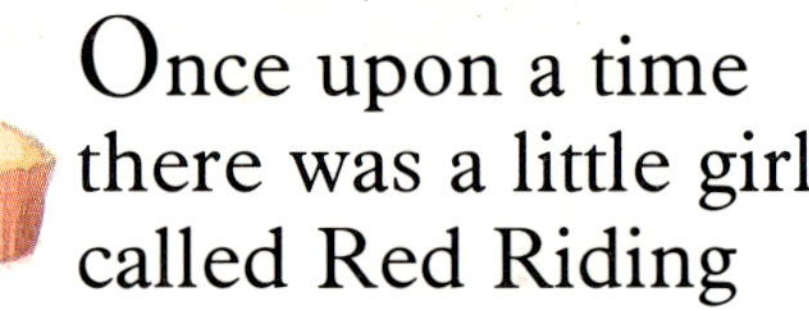

Once upon a time there was a little girl called Red Riding Hood. She always wore a red velvet cloak her grandmother had made for her. One day Red Riding Hood's grandmother was sick, so the little girl helped her mother bake lots of good things to make her grandmother well again.

Next day, Red Riding Hood set off early for her grandmother's cottage.

'Remember to keep to the path,' her mother said.

It was a long walk. The path went through a deep forest, between tall trees that cast shadows across every clearing.

Suddenly a big, bad wolf stepped out of the shadows.
'Hello, Red Riding Hood,' said the wolf.
'Hello, Mr Wolf,' she replied.
'Where are you going so early?' asked the wolf.
'To my grandmother's. She is sick and I am taking food to make her well again.'

'Where does your grandmother live?' the cunning wolf asked. Red Riding Hood pointed along the path.

Now the wolf had a wicked plan to eat up Red Riding Hood and her grandmother. 'Stop a while,' he said, 'and pick some pretty flowers for your poor grandmother.'

‘What a good idea,’ Red Riding Hood thought. So she left the path and wandered among the trees. Each time she picked a flower she saw a prettier one a little further on. She went deeper and deeper into the forest. Meanwhile, the wolf hurried on to the cottage.

Red Riding Hood's grandmother was lying in her upstairs bed when she heard the door knocker go RAT-A-TAT-TAT!
'Who's there?' she cried.
'Red Riding Hood,' said the wolf in his softest voice.
'Lift the latch and let yourself in,' said the grandmother.

Quickly, the wolf opened the door, climbed the stairs and gobbled up the poor old lady. Then he put on her nightdress. Next he put on her bonnet. And then he climbed into bed.

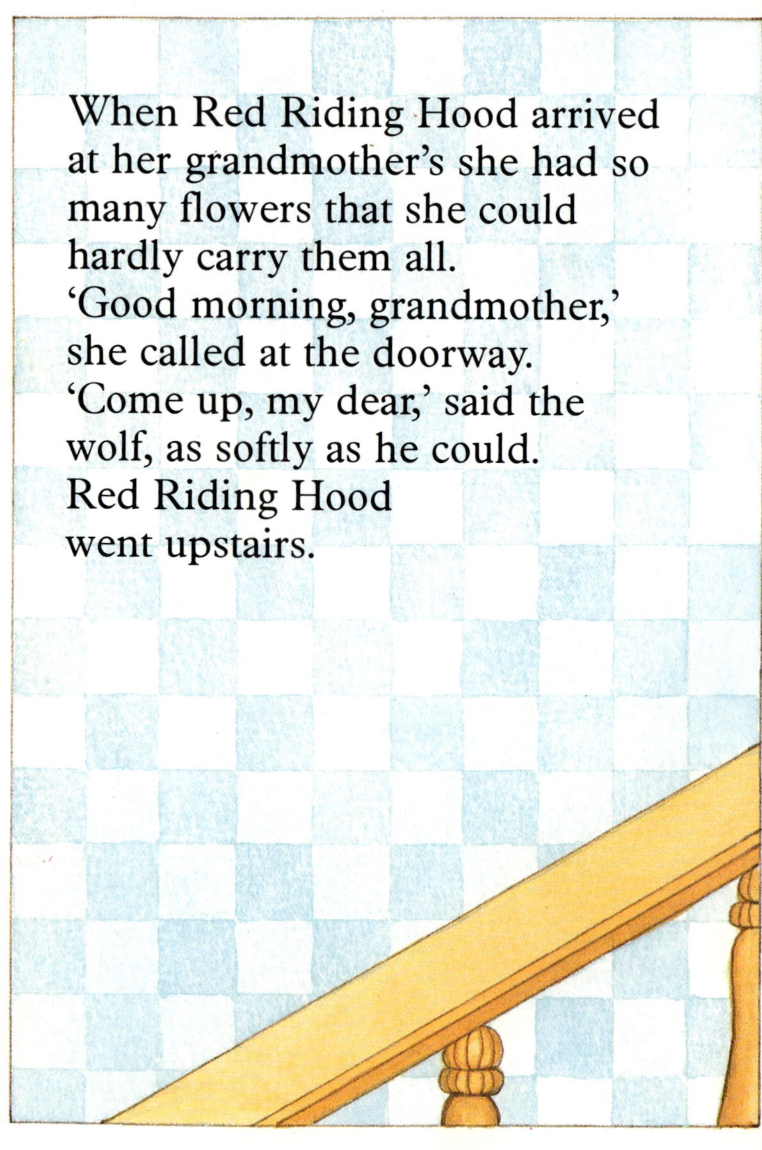

When Red Riding Hood arrived at her grandmother's she had so many flowers that she could hardly carry them all.
'Good morning, grandmother,' she called at the doorway.
'Come up, my dear,' said the wolf, as softly as he could.
Red Riding Hood went upstairs.

‘Oh, grandmother, what big ears you have!’ said Red Riding Hood. ‘All the better to hear you with, my dear!’ said the wolf.

‘And grandmother, what big eyes you have!’ said Red Riding Hood. ‘All the better to see you with, my dear!’ said the wolf.

'And what big teeth you've got!' said Red Riding Hood, coming close to the bedside.

'All the better to eat you with, my dear!' With those words the wolf sprang from under the bedclothes and swallowed Red Riding Hood in one gulp.

The wolf fell on the bed, full up with Red Riding Hood and her grandmother. Soon he was snoring so loudly that a passing hunter heard him.

'What a horrid snore for an old lady,' the hunter thought. He decided to go into the cottage to see if anything was wrong.

The hunter found the wolf fast asleep. ‘I’ve caught you at last!’ he cried. He killed the wicked animal immediately, then skinned it. To his surprise, out jumped Red Riding Hood.

‘How dark and frightening it was inside the wolf!’ she said.

Together, they helped the little girl’s grandmother out.

Everyone felt a lot better when they had eaten some of the food that Red Riding Hood had brought. Then the hunter took Red Riding Hood home.
From that day on, Red Riding Hood never wandered away from the path again, though she visited her grandmother lots of times.